Massive Power
Massive Love

Karl Ayling

Massive Power Massive Love by Karl Ayling

First Published in Great Britain in 2016

FAITHBUILDERS PUBLISHING www.biblestudiesonline.org.uk

An Imprint of Apostolos Publishing Ltd,

3rd Floor, 207 Regent Street,

London W1B 3HH

www.apostolos-publishing.com

British Library Cataloguing-in-Publication Data

A catalogue record for this book is available from the British Library

ISBN: 978-1-910942-21-5

Cover Design by Blitz Media, Pontypool, Torfaen

Cover Images © Siloto | Dreamstime.com

Printed and bound in Great Britain by Marston Book Services Limited, Oxfordshire.

Preface

Massive Power Massive Love

Healed and saved from above. The autobiographical book of Psalmic poems charting the journey of salvation and healing by the grace of the mercy of Jesus Christ

About the author

Karl Ayling was born in the village of Brixton in South West London and educated in that area. Born to parents who had lived as children through the atrocities of WW II—being separated from siblings and parents and the emotional impact of that experience—Karl grew up a fighter and lived life on the darker side in and around South London/North Surrey until the age of 41 when Jesus found him broken, dishevelled and suicidal. Suffering from Post-Traumatic Stress Disorder and twice divorced, what did God want with this stray from the wrong side of the tracks?

Introduction

Taking the reader through a fifty year journey towards salvation and subsequent healing, this book charts God's tender loving care in transforming a sex addict suffering from (undiagnosed) Obsessive Compulsive Disorder and Post Traumatic Stress Disorder in a series of individual poetic segments. The product of two broken families and in a self-contained exile of spiritual, emotional, physical, mental and financial poverty, Karl Ayling takes the reader through three key aspects of a transforming life: Healing, Forgiveness and Relationships. These look at how God's grace and mercy gradually healed and restored him to physical, spiritual, mental and emotional health.

How do we as human beings limit ourselves? How do negative emotions cause destructive fallout that requires transformational thinking? Does the focus on past events prevent us from fully experiencing God's still and gentle love for us? Are you scared of being brilliant and amazing? Consumed by negative thinking?

The journey is ongoing and a number of counsellors, ministers, doctors, family, friends and loved ones have all contributed greatly to the healing. This has included a learning of love and a learning to love alongside the setting of boundaries that are the influence of Christ in this one life.

Special Thanks

The early draft of this book was written in long hand over the summer and winter of 2013 and into 2014. The people of Caffe Nero's Banstead deserve a mention for letting me enjoy very good coffee and a comfortable environment in which to work.

Also, there were those from my home church who encouraged me to pick up a pen and get started in the first place, to start writing – thank you.

Prayer

Daddy fill me up with love and cuddles as deep as the ocean, come dwell with me, laugh with me, rest with me, teach me, heal me. Thank you in Jesus' name. Amen

NB – Daddy = Heavenly Father God. Abba = Heavenly Father God

Contents

SECTION 1: MASSIVE POWER, MASSIVE LOVE

SECTION 2: HEALED AND SAVED

SECTION 1

MASSIVE POWER, MASSIVE LOVE

FUTURE MYSTERY

Since I can remember, the killer had tried to place my history into my future.

But I have a testimony, a blessing from Heaven that makes my future a mystery.

Under His blood is my history and the light shines only at my feet.

The liar minces between half-truths to confuse, but light defeats night and right prevails.

That last fateful step into darkness is averted;

To the abyss I am alerted.

He tugs me back away from death and gives me a future filled with love and cuddles, smiles,

And miles of blissful walks, talks and Happy Valley vistas.

And a peace that defies history—future mystery.

AIR I BREATHE

I believe He made the trees, the flowers, He made me and He made you.

He made the birds of the air—yes those too.

He made the air that I breathe and the fish of the sea.

He made darkness and He made light.

He gives healing and blots out my transgressions—

My scarlet sin, so crimson—

And He restores me to love.

The liar is defeated; he bleats meekly.

The stars tell of a cosmic glory sensed yet unseen by eyes of man.

I believe He made me—made me to shine forth a light that He has placed within me.

Quiet and bright, mine to shine, mine to keep,

A deposit of the promise made by His word to show the way in this world.

As I curl to sleep He is mine and I am His to keep with pictures, words, dreams.

He teaches, corrects, and directs by love.

He increases me to be all that He made me to be.

MASSIVE POWER

Massive power, massive love, healed and saved

From above

By a love I did not earn

That holds me near both night and day.

Through the ups and downs, when feeling down

And burdened by my tarnished crown;

It's always there come rain or shine,

Through a promise true that makes it mine.

A love so true I cannot say a word or thing to lose its way.

Massive power, massive love, healed and saved

From above

By my Father's love—

Abba Father's love.

ANGEL LIGHT

Angels can fly because they take and hold everything lightly.

Light breathes life into everything.

Is this why they visit us at night, delivering Daddy's blessings and lessons at the quietest time?

Could you cope with a single touch at any other time?

Would your mind comprehend— their touch is so light as to be imperceptible?

Would this rescue you from calamity of work, calamity of family, calamity of spouse, calamity of life?

Have we missed the glory, the mercy, the joy, the love of His tender touch by the breadth of a hair?

Have I blinked out of synchronisation with the Creator's rhythm?

Does my heart not jump elatedly when the angel's delivery finds its target?

Lord provide me an angel's light.

FATHER'S LOVE

As long as the thunder roars and the north wind blows.

As long as the rain falls.

As long as the mountains tremble and the lightning flashes across the skies.

As long as the sun shines.

As long as the moon is full and the high tide rolls; while the rivers flow.

As long as the snow is cold.

As long as the grass is green and the stars burn; while the universe turns.

As long as black holes consume and the oceans breathe.

As long as the earth has been is as long as you have loved me, kept me, saved me, kissed me, known me, planned me.

As long as the day lingers, come dwell with me. As long as I have breath, join me.

As long as you say, I will be here.

DIG THE CREATOR

I dig the sound of the ocean.

I dig the pebbles at the beach. I dig the sun on my face.

I dig a cooling breeze. I dig bird-sound.

I dig the smell of ground coffee. I dig hugs and kisses.

I dig my Daddy's love.

I dig the threshing floor. I dig wide blue skies.

I dig smiles that touch the eyes.

I dig Galatians 5 and Ephesians 5. I dig your word.

I dig the sunset.

I dig the Surrey hills.

I dig creation in all its glory. I dig the creator.

I dig the promise and its fulfilment. I dig the moon at night.

I dig the Canis Majoris.

I dig puppies chasing their tails. I dig Laninin.

BEAUTY IN YOU

The beauty in your dominion draws out the awe,

The creative, the love in me—yes that too.

The sheer size of Mauni Karua boggles the mind as it reflects the glory of your divine creation.

Like a full moon rising, reflecting off a calm, turning tide at the oceans edge.

The splendour of the Blue Mountains under a cover of snow

And the sweltering heat of the southern tip of the Grand Canyon;

Optical illusions floating on the haze:

You are more real.

It is your heart teaching mine:

Devotion, integrity, faithfulness.

Each moment I'm here is yours.

Nothing, no nothing, happens without your presence

And I catch my breath in the glorious beauty of you.

LIGHT HORIZON

There is a place south of Croydon where on a clear dark night a cross can be seen from afar.

It gleams as if suspended from Heaven with no visible means of support.

The light shines my Lord's glory showing it to all who cast their eye above the horizon.

Just as God's unseen, majestic hand guides me with a lamp to my feet, this light provides a serene comfort.

Then, by the light of the day, the eye can see high up on a hill close to Farthing Down;

A turret atop a church reaching up like God's own lighthouse—free for all to marvel at.

Such as these are Daddy's blessings, free to all who want to see Him, seek Him and ask.

Father prompt me each day to ask you for all things.

HAND MADE

My conception was not some random event, but an orchestrated celestially planned one.

I am seeking, finding and working out my purpose.

I have been delayed by a convoluted pathway strewn with missed opportunities to find salvation.

A new heart, a new mind and a real peace have been gifted

As spiritual, emotional, physical, mental, and financial health and well-being

Permit a walk of divine health.

Though evil walks and stalks around every corner,

At night, awake,

Green eyes piercing the dawn;

Heart beating away like a bass drum,

I turn and a rhythmic breathing flows back, blissful safety.

Rejoice, rejoice warrior angels and claim the ground.

Rest deepens, what concerns?

FAITH, HOPE & LOVE

There are banners hanging from the roof

Of a church in a beautiful shade of blue.

They declare; Faith, Hope and Love.

The greatest of these is love, for love triumphs over all.

Lord I ask that you remind me daily to forgive injuries, both perceived and real.

I give thanks for your great love that first chased me, wooed me, courted me and eventually captured me,

Turning my heart away from the deepest darkness.

As the blades of grass fade and wither so the fragile human frame declines and complies with your great design.

So that one day we will come face to face and know there has already been atonement for all my transgressions.

Till that time I choose to embrace your grace and mercy,

And give thanks with a humble heart for the love that so tenderly holds me.

JUST DON'T KNOW

One thing I have learned, or two;

I can no more determine a man's tribulations than I can predict when the fruit of a horse chestnut tree will fall.

I do know that it falls, but the precise moment that it falls is known only to you, for you know all things.

Such is the abject countenance of myself and my fellow man; all mysteries are known only to God.

My very apparent limitations are designed to persuade me, to ask questions, and seek the answers from the maker of the stars.

A limited viewer can only wonder at the mystery of its creator

And fall deeply in love at the wonder of His creation.

Nothing new under the sun has ever been formed, all purpose is found only in Him—

In the gaze of His loving eye, seeing all, knowing all; from which nothing is ever hidden.

NEVER FAR

He didn't meet with me at a well in the noon day sun.

He showed me a series of pictures that He was there with me at the moment of conception, with a glimpse of my parents' emotional state at the time.

Valuable revelation. He showed me He was there at my birth, holding me, protecting me from the beginning.

He waited for me to fall into the Father's outstretched hand.

He was there when I was thrown like a rag doll against a wall, head cracking plaster, urine pouring out of me;

Yes, He was there, keeping me sane.

He was there preserving me for salvation when my childhood was being stripped away. He was there to reassure, encourage and protect.

When they all said 'He'll be OK', was the sentence he served enough?

Have I forgiven enough?

Love swells like a swollen river.

Overflows, pours out when I least expect it. So, maybe, yes—enough is enough.

SURRENDERED YET?

The warrior's heart and mind surrender to the prospect of battle and prepare him with ruthless efficiency.

Just as an athlete trains and hardens his body by repeating the same moves over and over again, excellence emerges over time.

Transferring the same discipline and processes to seeking the Father's heart and teaching develops (over time) a surrendered life.

A divine infilling of that God-shaped hole in the heart and a divine, abundant, celestial, peaceful, indwelling emerges.

There is a correlation to surrenderedness that determines the beauty of the garden and the fruit that it is capable of producing.

Filtration of the toxic streams produces abundance.

It is not mere knowledge of the truth that sets you free,

For the heart to be transformed it must first be surrendered.

Surrendered yet?

NO, YES

Halitosis is something that you can smell;

Integrity is something that you can tell.

You can see it by its presence;

You can discern its absence.

You can compromise it, you can refine it, you can ask for an increase,

You can practice it and then in an instant let it slip.

Keeping it accesses immense fulfilment.

Plugging into the source trips open a galaxy held in place by the giving and keeping of a word.

Never compromised, never changed. You may run from it but you can never hide,

Everything is seen. The giving of a word contains power,

The keeping of it bestows resources,

The breaking of it, calamity.

As a river discharges into the sea, integrity ebbs and flows through us; establishing peace and contentment.

PATIENCE ROCK

Father God,

Sit me on the rock to await your infilling of me and the land around me.

Bring green pastures anew and meadows that cause life to flourish.

Grant me the grace to await your refinement,

And when the time is done and you are satisfied bring forth the fulfilment of your promise.

Let love establish itself when it is good and ready.

Enabled, stable, and of a suitable foundation based upon Jesus' might and not on mine.

Let your kingdom come, your will be done in all things.

Let surrender reach all aspects of my life.

Be the only source of life as you reveal more of yourself to me.

BLESSINGS AND LESSONS

I have learned to give thanks for being born in England;

A land where free school and free school milk helped to generate strong bones.

There is good clean water to drink straight from the tap and there has been all of my life.

Cadbury's chocolate is made in England; no other is worth trying, trust me.

Triumph makes my favourite bikes in England, the north Downs Hills, Banstead Woods, and Brighton are all nearby.

Well, there's the M25 too and leaves that fall in October,

Rain almost every month, wind, sun in July and snow in January.

Sometimes the trains don't work and the airports are closed when it snows.

Never mind! Aren't we safer in London than we are in L.A. or NYC or Jo'Berg?

I have learned that forgiving mother, matters too.

Resting in the rock matters, what I see, what I hear, what I say, matters a lot too.

LONELY IN LONDON

As a child it was lonely for me in Treelawn Road
where the edginess of existence came closest to
penetrating the life that I was given.

The knives and the guns, that have claimed so many
sons, passed me by.

The rock of my salvation found me, not in the obvious
places or the snowy powder evident on every cistern
in town.

But, I found Him whilst checking the stop watch as I
ran.

Running in flight from dark, hopefully into light.

Hearing the call that saved a life.

Learning late that poverty is as much a state of mind,

Keeping me empty inside.

Then, slowly the evidence of the poverty of the lonely
was shared by one true friend, who cared more for me
than I did;

He opened my eyes, woke me up to what was inside.

Loneliness flies away by day and by night, tenderly
held in the angels' delight.

MY HEART

Do you hear my cry by day and by night?

You shelter me under your great wing and bring persecution.

Else how would I know to turn this way, or that, from my iniquity to the King?

My soul longs, waits to see your face.

You hide me from the plots and the dangerous rebellion of the world and its stinking minions.

Quench my dryness, slake my thirst, guard my mouth, my ears, my eyes, my heart

—for trouble resides within my heart.

Help me, embrace, let no evil reach me nor my ear hear of it.

Let me trust only in you at all times; pouring out my heart into the safety of your refuge.

As the sun rises in the morning we shall praise you and rejoice.

I seek your wisdom, O my rock, my defender, my salvation, my expectation, my provider, my heart.

DISCOVERY

Everything that I do impacts eternity.

I discovered a song called Love Reign O'er Me at age thirteen and only realized that it was meant for my salvation forty years later. Rain on me.

I discovered women at about the same time as motor cycles. Motor cycles are more faithful.

I discovered that I hate fakery and fakery hates me.

I discovered scuba diving and sky diving on the way to discovering you;

And, a love of chess and creativity.

At twenty-eight and thirty-one the boys were born to different mothers. I discovered how to love outside my own anatomy.

I've discovered that waiting can be better than rushing.

Asking Daddy to hold my hand my heart helps me to detect the eternal aspect.

Broken relationships show me how far there is yet to go.

I have discovered God doesn't mind who I choose to marry, but that I choose positively, deferring to, and transforming into Him.

DEVIL PREVAILS

As I close my eyes to reflect, I can detect the lies the enemy has told. Did you know that there are as many miraculous healings in Europe as there are in Africa?

The Islamists have given up on taking the Dark Continent because each time God heals a voodoo doctor or tribal leader a church gets planted and grows.

A man called Surprise oversees these miracles and has planted over eight hundred churches in the darkest places of Africa.

There is a simple reason why there is no credible, clear revival; the dark one devours good news and corrupts its messengers.

Don't we all collect our idols and submit to addictions, negativity, and corruption, without for a moment considering that our responsibility, accountability or integrity are under great threat?

Let me tell you something, my friend, to lose weight you need do only two things: eat less and exercise more. That's it. Job done.

What does the world tell you? No magazine column and no book can do it for you; it's all a lie. If you imbibe too much alcohol, any drugs, or tobacco, you are making a death wish and you will pay for it, spiritually, physically, mentally, and financially. God has given you the choice—you choose.

EARLY DAZE

As a child I was beautiful, handsome, easy on the eye; a good looking kid.

The children at school wouldn't take me as second, third or fourth string—rejected.

Getting beaten up, robbed, and mugged was normal.

Sitting with the doghouse blues, I too was born with nothing and I've still got most of it left.

Naming me Steve for the first couple of weeks, dad came back from registering the birth and had called me Karl, after Marx.

Dad wasn't having a lark, he really was that far left.

He wanted a reminder of his learning, they have no meaning these days.

I hold on to the cross, he'd vehemently disapprove.

Loving what Jesus did on the cross teaches me to engage with the lost, the beaten.

Starting with me and working from inside out, teaching me to accept humanity's brokenness;

A reason to love, a reason to live on. Stop choking on the dust of hatred, supping on poisonous streams of toxicity and animosity, filling life with deathly putrid things.

PHYSICAL PARTICLES

I let my gaze lift up to the moon, draw my shoulders back, and wonder at this wide, wide creation.

Not just a nation under the stars; the particles that make up me and you can be found running around free at the outer reaches of the universe.

See, there is no intellect capable of seeing the infinite creativity that holds this all in place.

But, the way that the moon draws earth's tides this way,

Hints at an order beyond human comprehension.

On a stormy May Day, as the ground shakes and the earth flexes its muscles,

The anger in the earth just hints at the shaking winds that blow throughout the universe as Daddy exhales over His creation,

It's in our nature to seek to try to fill that space.

But it is hopeless without His breath.

PSALM 83

I have little wisdom. For some the blindness will remain for an eternity.

Those who become lost do so despite God making them an exit route.

A whirling wind in the dust; stars shine to show the way.

Fires burn and set the mountains on fire.

Am I all you stood for?

Pursue them with your gentle tempest till they know your name and shout it out.

Enlighten them with your storms until their wandering becomes a wondering.

Fill their faces with shame till they seek your name,

Till they know that you alone sit on the throne high over the earth, willing to save them before they drown.

Confounded and dismayed,

Don't keep silent as the violent

Take counsel against those that love you.

Give us the courage to sing.

DESPONDENCY

Unite my heart till I fear your name.

Let my thoughts be nimble with competing interests.

Even the demons believe in you and quiver at your name.

The 'God particle' confounds man's minds; yet it points the way to you.

As I cry out, I waste away because of my afflictions, heavy with convictions.

So, I stretch my hands out to you and ask that you be merciful.

Why is my soul cast off, why do you hide your face from me?

My youth has afflicted me; I suffer and am distraught—

Waters engulf me, my loved ones and friends have abandoned me and have been put far from me.

Forgive me; I contemplate my iniquities and find that their number is too great to count.

Oh, how greatly I have grieved you, yet you clothe me in your righteousness.

RAPTURE

Oh my Lord! I yearn for your rapture!

Let me not remain here in the rupturedness of life,

Where I drown in the iniquities of my enemies and the activities of the dark one overtake.

I am driven to my knees, my eyes heavenward.

Please, do not forsake me, remember my frailty.

My heart longs for you though it is scarlet in sin.

Let your mercies renew me each day, let me dwell in your house, let your Spirit comfort me.

Release me from the terror of the threat of separation,

For alone I cannot tame the animal nature that lurks seeking to devour me.

Send me a helper, to keep the gate, to purify the waters which I sup.

Cleanse me to enable me to reflect the glory of your transforming love.

HOLY SPIRIT GRIEVING

Spoiler alert! There is no such thing as generational sin. Deuteronomy 24 v16, Ezekiel 18 v14–21, Jeremiah 31 v29 and John 9 v1–3 give His word.

Then Isaiah 53 declares that we are healed by His stripes.

Yet, as Abba Father breathes life abundant into me, I know I have grieved the Holy Spirit by preaching falsely.

Grant me redemption for my sin and increase my wisdom and discernment to your word which are your gifts.

Lord my heart grieves at the ungodly teaching and preaching that I adopted in your great name that has put judgement above mercy.

Is this why outpouring is so profoundly present at my home church?

Every ministry steeped and built on the lie that generational sin pervades will fall.

Lord show me the light to see your plans for me in that place.

Thank you for your close encounters for the rejoicing of your people.

STRONGHOLD

Do I have a case; is there any solution to the pollution afflicting me and touching the whole human race?

Do my eyes, my ears, my mouth, my heart deceive me?

Do I permit myself to dwell upon ungodly obsession?

Addicted to the flesh, to idolatry that reeks,

Even after the application of a waterfall of cleansing water.

I can try to hide from His sight, the plight that I fight

In my own puny might.

Any child may see right

Through me.

The chains are slipping off I am breaking free,

Gradually.

No faster than I can stand, no more on shifting sand.

Awaiting impatiently for that moment when she will come and slip her hand into mine.

Never really ready and yet ever ready;

Honed responses detect the presence of the present awaited.

CHEAP HONESTY

As the snow falls and settles upon the ground, my soul is purified and I ask my groaning heart,

'How long have I got to go before the sun comes out?'

Please don't tell me that you love me, I'm not sure I'm ready to say it back to you this time.

I was singing a song, sheep on a stick, for the longest time,

Before a glance at the lyric sheet informed me that the line was actually Cheap Honesty.

Reminding me of the one who deals in death through cheap honesty, who rapes children, corrupts souls, and kills.

Giving us 80% of the truth in a matter; only to bring the crushing revelation that the other 20% is what will destroy us,

Taking us like a bull led by its nose down into the pit, the highway to hell.

Cheap honesty is all around,

An unavoidable part of the fabric of the world's corruption—oozing out of every orifice.

It was cheap honesty that was the cause of Eve eating the forbidden fruit. Death entered the world.

The neon enticements of the kingdom of darkness send you and me a strong signal to turn to the one true light to discern His presence, His love in every temptation.

To boldly seek the light that has been knit into us all; desiring to fill the meaningless emptiness with the lifesaving word of God.

A warning echoes, bouncing off the wall each time we step outside the protection of the Father's light.

Cheap honesty can be a vile tool for blinding, for misdirection—encouraging the flesh to flare up in lustful disobedience.

Leading us to a torment that our in-built judgements,

Assessments and opinions try to justify, they count as nothing.

If your judgement is not triumphed by mercy, forget telling me that you love me pastor, show me you love me.

I have learned the language of love so that we can converse together from the heart,

Come and talk to me and I will show you that I love you too.

Leave the sheep on a stick to graze in the wilderness, roaming in the dark; don't bring it home with you to bring desolation. Don't.

CYCLING

A complicated contradiction of complex issues that daily ebb and flow in importance.

Priorities wane as the mood takes; slipping so easily from a foundational equilibrium of love towards the abyss.

It amazes that the predictability of the fall cannot somehow be halted, even for a season.

Despite the cycle of inevitability, linked to the moons;

Turning only to Jesus, who rebuked the wind and the heaving seas, for him to quieten the shrew voices—by His miracle to intercede.

The flesh explodes like a volcano, pouring out its poison in all directions,

Only the Holy Spirit can rescue the afflicted,

Piercing through the lava like an armour piercing round,

Bringing peace in the place of the chaos.

Only by a miracle—by the Fathers love—can the cycle of destruction be halted and the effects reversed, by forgiveness.

Bring your requests to the foot of the cross where anger abates. Amen.

SURROUNDED

Know that you have not been swallowed alive or swept away.

As you pass though rapids you have not been overwhelmed,

Surrounded or captured for too long in the snare of a flower's perfume.

The teeth of the devourer's gnash miss their target, yet escape was not mine; it was a gift of divine intervention.

By His allowance, my soul emerges intact,

As the mountains surround me, so Zion surrounds me,

Reminding me that I am frail and flighty.

His almighty wing enfolds me as I lay down my life for heavens cause.

He builds His kingdom right here, within me.

His love engulfs me from this time forth and for evermore.

He has done great things for those that sow in tears,

They will dance with rejoicing and shall reap a reward in deep joy.

HEDGING

The Lord will perfect that which concerns me, And that which concerns me the Lord will make perfect.

For He has searched me and discerns my heart. I can say nothing that He has not already foretold.

He runs before me and after me, He is my protection. His hand is upon me.

Wherever I go His Spirit finds me there. What use is there in hiding as under His wings I dwell.

I am known from the most inner parts, light is all around,

Surrounding me since I was conceived in the womb,

Your love, your love has engulfed me.

My soul knows your presence and your grieving; too much grieving.

In your book were all my days recorded before a single one was seen.

Precious are your thoughts toward me. Vast in number are the blessings you bestow upon me.

Do I not detest those of the world who take your name in vain? Search me and know my anxieties.

WARRIOR

When I resist emotional disappointment, joy
evaporates; along with the death of my desires.

Like the pain of a dislocated elbow, I scream out in
shock that I have found myself walking around the
same mountain again.

Courage was not mediated to me in the womb or in
the family where He placed me.

I have learned that His love alone is worthy of all of
the fight that I have.

Using a warrior's instinct sparingly, restless
abandonment prevails. Eternity rests only in the
present,

He said look for me and you will find me.

There is no compromise where I'm looking.

Where I choose to hide, I repel the love that I crave—

Just like a hand in a glove is comfortable yet
desensitised.

It is dark there, dead to any intricate sensations.

My rejection goes back to conception.

My participation is a requisite to receiving restoration.

His betrothal to me, mine to Him.

PURIFY

Remember Proverbs 8 – the oxen is led by its nose ring to work and unto death.

Beauty has the power to ensnare us and to walk us down the highway to darkness and into hell.

The lust of the flesh and the loneliness of the long distance runner must become reconciled to love in all its purity.

Only the water of the Holy Spirit's purity can deeply slake the thirst and put out the burning of the fire.

Let the water level rise, Lord; let my well run deep and pure let me sup only of its cool fragrant, life-giving qualities.

Grant that your great wisdom and deep understanding are refreshed within me daily.

That we are not forsaken in times of trouble and mess.

Be my guide, be my protection,

Be my significant companion from this day forth and for evermore.

Let my eye gaze upon you, chin up, elevated above the horizon—renewed in wisdom and purity.

WHAT A SECOND CHANCE

He will make beautiful the humble with salvation,

As we praise His Holy name and give thanks for His restoration.

Praise Him with your life; praise Him with your voice.

A second chance would see me dead already, used up, washed away.

How could I rejoice and praise from the dust?

So, He gives me air to breath and I dance by fire light.

Knowing that soon He will turn all things to good for those that love Him.

Trust Him with all my heart, learning not to lean on my own limited understanding.

Resting in His assurance as He directs my paths.

There wasn't much to figure out, invigoration comes when I let go of myself,

Get out of the way of progress and let Him take command of my days.

Praise His mighty hand of love.

SECTION 2

HEALED AND SAVED

SHINE LIGHT SHINE

When you build a fire, you start off with paper and small twigs and dry grasses. Once the flame is built you add larger twigs, then branches, then logs. Once alive the fire brings warmth and light and security, the creatures of the night will not come near, nor those that would devour.

In the same way it is your blessing to kindle the Father's fire within you, to bring forth its light, heat and radiance, protection and security. Thus a light shines that attracts and repels those who are not blind to the Fathers love.

He brings forth healing with a glimpse of the Kingdom of heaven. If you feed a fire with the things a fire needs to burn you will keep its light burning. Equally, if you feed it things that reduce it, it will snuff out and eventually die.

Even then our great God will resurrect from the ashes the kindle of a new flame. He will not forsake us or leave us in the cold for long. His warmth is there, glowing like the embers waiting to be fed nourishing feed. We all need nourishing for death awaits around the corner, waiting for those asleep in the grass, waiting to wither, waiting to die—will this grass bring forth a light that will banish the night?

NAKED I AM

Planned from the dawn of time, known from the moment of conception; I am known to Him.

Naked I am.

Every moment I have had and am yet to have are known only to Him. Naked I am.

Every lie I have told. Every secret I hold are known to Him. Naked I am.

He gives me the desires of my heart. And He threshes away that which must go. Naked I am

If it's surrendered He knows, if it's not, He knows. He's Alpha and He's Omega.

Naked I am.

Every penny I stole is counted. All the times I have fallen He has discounted. Naked I am.

All gifts. All woes. All blessings and all lessons are from Him. Naked I am.

He is love. He is peace. He is wisdom. He is hope. Naked I am.

But I am known to him.

THERE HE IS

From the moment that the egg was reached He was there.

Through growth, development and birth, He was there.

When they counted toes and smacked my bottom and tickled my nose,

He was there.

Through the silent screams of those early years, He was there.

When my face was slapped and my childhood crushed, He was there.

From the discovery of Reign O'er Me in '73 till the revelation of its meaning in my life in 2013, He was there.

Through all of the rain on me, He was there.

He taught me to love and receive love.

He turned deathly resignation into transformational restoration.

He showed me Yahweh is the way.

Through lessons and blessings, He peeled away the layers of sorrows and of loss to show me His peace and His joy.

He takes me by the hand and explains about the promised land.

His word transcends my comprehension. His love never ends.

He teaches me that I am a husband from the moment that you meet me and that I am your husband from the moment that you marry me.

He teaches me that nothing happens without His say so.

The Holy Spirit whispers wisdom and guidance

And I yearn to discern the lightness from the turbulence of the night;

Darkness recedes.

A yielded heart cries out for the Father's touch

And when I am alone and fearful there He is.

When I run, when I used the phone to look at images I don't own, there He is turning my ashes into beauty.

There He is, there He is, do you see, there He is.

FOUND YOU

I have searched, oh how I have searched.

In London, Edinburgh, Inverness, yes even Lands'
End and John O'Groats,

Paris, Rome, Nice, Copenhagen, Hamburg, Bruges,

Holland, at the top of Mount Tiedi, Athens, Rhodes,
Kos

And the search went to Los Angeles, San Francisco,

Right down the Mississippi, San Diego,

Plant City, Atlanta, Singapore, Malaysia, Bangkok, the
Gold Coast,

Sydney, Cairns, and the Great Barrier reef on the
ocean floor—

These and others bought me no relief from the grief.

Not jumping out of planes, or speeding on race tracks
@166,

Not sex, not drugs, not rock and roll; not running, not
hiding.

You found me, desperate to answer your call, the
rainbow chasing ceased. Your faith released life.

ALIVE

Alive! I am alive!

At three with pee falling down over my knees.

I am alive at seven when the paternal rapist departs
leaving me in the hands of the maternal abuser.

Alive at eighteen with a Potts fracture, crutches and a
close encounter at twenty-two with the Moonie cult in
California.

Alive after a desert smash up in Arizona, I am alive.

Slipping out of a plane at 400 feet, rescued to complete
the feat.

Despite no protection, completely in the wrong
direction, I am still alive!

I have made it this far;

He is guiding and transforming my way.

The darkness recedes, never really leaves,

There's time, just a little longer, and space for the star
maker,

The cosmic mover and shaker, to keep me alive in
you.

GOD'S HEALING GRACE

By His unfailing love, my sight was saved.

Migraines have abated and diseases have fled.

By nothing that man has done, my back is healed—

Thank you Lord.

The fog in the mind has lifted, Post-Traumatic Stress Disorder shifted.

Replaced by peace with myself, peace with my community;

Peace with my friends and peace with God too.

He has taken away a life and given me another.

There is less Obsessive Compulsive Disorder to oppress me,

Just a deeper sense of contentment and an overwhelming presence of His love.

Now, He is sending me a gatekeeper to keep me company on this journey;

A blessing beyond measure.

MY GARDEN

The garden has been cleared of interlopers and trespassers—

The boundary secured against unwelcome entry.

The river flows freely and the waterfall filters and purifies,

Offering a serene place to soak in His presence.

Surrounded by willow trees and flowers in blossom, the scents of spring on the air.

An expanse of blue sky reflects the hue of the oceans.

The butterflies and the birds frolic on the gentle breeze.

The shade of the rocks bring relief from the heat of the day and offers a covering where in the slumber the spirit imparts its wondrous comfort.

Meadows stretch out as far as the eye can see,

Offering rolling hills to delight the sight of my garden.

SHADES AND HUES

The wonder of the autumn shades strike me,

As the trees turn from greens and yellows and purples into browns.

The green represents new life, a new life that is available only through you,

The purple represents the robes of the prince that you have dressed me in;

Me! The undeserving soul who does that which he wishes not to do; and does not do that which he wishes to do.

As the temperature of the days turn from summer heat to autumn cool, your glory is revealed and my heart sings.

The stars shine ever so brightly in the crisp night sky and the moon gives of its guiding light.

Be my guide, guide me where you would have me to be. I will watch and see till I hear Thee.

HIGHER PLACE

From the turret of a castle the enemy can be seen approaching,

Whether in stealth in the night or in the bright light of the day.

As the eagle soars high on unseen thermals so my watcher looks to who approaches.

Ordering my footsteps to avoid calamity—how can the unhealed hope to accommodate the unhealed? This is a calamity unfolding!

How have we been saved from a low vantage point by that still small whisper?

No, not here, not me, not this one, I'm closing my eyes to listen,

The gift of a new spirit-name calls;

Soaring Beauty.

Soar beauty, use your gift to hear, touch, taste, see and sense that which you are called to sense.

He guides you to helpful things from His vantage point on high.

Seeing things not seen on the ground, seeing what lurks around the corner waiting to ensnare, to kill and to destroy.

MERCY SHINES

Although I am a speck of dust on a grain of sand I believe that by the mighty power of my Father in Heaven a purpose is emerging.

Gradually revealed,

Slowly taking shape in this lifetime.

Day by day His still small voice tells me that though my sin runs crimson and I am soaked in the tainted filth of this world,

He has called me and saved me.

He has written my name in the book of life.

By His blood I am purified, not by any works that I have done, but by His grace.

Oh how I long for my brothers and sisters to detect the heart and see the light that brings life eternal.

Oh how I give thanks for my new heart, my new mind, my healing.

Thank you Daddy.

WITHOUT YOU

I know that without you I would be on the way to a white stick and a guide dog.

Without you I would be dead; with you, through you, I live.

Without you I would be poisoned by the Moonies, a vegetable.

Without you I would be holding on to a simmering hatred of my mother and father.

Without you I would not have found Nemo at the bottom of the Great Barrier Reef.

Without you that car crash would have taken my life in Phoenix

And without your miracles I would not be saved.

Without you my son would not be seeking the light.

Without you the spiritual, physical, emotional pain would be unbearable.

I soar with you.

CLOSE ENCOUNTERS

A smartly dressed man in a security uniform offered me sex for one English pound in an Indian airport; but what price HIV?

What price dignity? What price poverty? What price life?

I know what it feels like to ride a motorcycle at 267KPH, pull a wheelie at 236KPH and survive to tell the tale.

Only now, however, do I know that it was no skill of mine that preserved me; I was indifferent to life.

From a deep financial calamity, business collapsed, marriages collapsed, house gone, material things gone;

God stripped all things away, establishing sovereignty over all things.

He stirred a purpose in me, prepared the man for a perspective bigger than one single broken view.

He took the mould, broke it and blew off the dust, destroyed the comfort zones, cleared the eyes, opened the heart for heavenly purposes;

Instilled a thirst for His life that was absent since birth. He's taken my gaze upward, increased me.

SUDDENLY

From the smack of the back of his hand to the welts from the belt in her hand,

An early sense of voided love was deeply engraved into the soul.

Three was too soon to know the hurt and the hate would never go.

It was only with divine intervention that I could learn to know how to show love.

Tricksy flipping from pillar to post never filled or healed that sickening void,

Violence and myriad forms of death never lifted the clinging fog.

Not until a healing prayer ministry showed me the key, like the apple falling from a tree,

It suddenly occurred to me that I was free by grace divine.

Free to be me, free not to flee, free to feel the awe of my Father's immense love and expansive creation.

Not just a nation, not just a planet, much, much bigger than that.

Salvation came. Daddy I love you.

MEANINGLESS

There are many things that appear to give meaning to life, but Solomon says that life is meaningless. And it is meaningless that it is meaningless.

As we are pushed from the womb, we seek meaning and purpose, but life brings no answer on its own, just a steady push back to the dust from whence we came.

What did it mean to me to slip from a plane that banked a bit too sharply, to be rescued from a fall at a few hundred feet—meaningless.

It took another seemingly more mundane reason to stop me from jumping out of airplanes.

I learned that I was there when they crucified my Lord,

I helped draw the spear that had the crowd cheer and roar,

As His blood and waters ran clear.

Now, in the horror of the complicity of my role I seek salvation for my soul,

I feel the need to fill the hole with a grace filled purpose,

Designed to make me whole;

As He intended.

Spirit-filled devotion, love, hope, and faith now bring me a new sense of purpose.

I find movies meaningless, thrills meaningless, music meaningless, travel meaningless; sex, drugs and rock and roll are meaningless—

Everything in meaningless until the Spirit opens my eyes to see the vision

And my ears to hear the Creator's hand in all things.

Only then does the wonder of all things release their true meaning to a man in his pitiful, short period of meaningless existence.

God knows that the dead cannot praise Him

So He prompts us, guides us, whispers to us, sends us, encounters us to challenge us;

Gives us a choice to look beyond our pitiful, short period of meaningless existence

To the wonder and meaning of 'Christ in us'.

DESOLATE AFFLICTED

Desolate and afflicted, when did the isolation end?

Has the influence of the filth of the world begun to dissolve?

Afflicted by toxic friends and lovers for an eternity,

In human terms, supping streams of toxicity.

Afflicted and gripped by addictions to sexuality, physicality,

And compulsions to extremities that end in bloody desolation.

Fragmented, broken, fragments of fragments;

Too many to pick up, too many to piece together;

Too overwhelmed to gauge the beginning from the end.

There is One that is truly beautiful; His beauty replaces my ashes,

Transforming the desolate affliction, making the divine exchange: death for life; hate for love; hope for hopelessness; faith for faithlessness.

GARDEN OF LIFE

As vision clears, that which has been planted in the garden can more clearly be seen.

The abundance of choking weeds and brambles detected;

Defects in the boundary corrected.

Undesirable presences ejected,

Rotten smells and corruptions disinfected,

Clouds lifted and hills shifted. And lo, life begins to return.

As the soil is sifted first fruits appear, the streams purify and an abundance is available.

Pastures emerge, lush and green, as far as the eye can see.

Clean pools and waterfalls offer an infilling of spiritual cleansing,

Silt is sifted, well-springs teem with life.

Unseen seed produces fruit, fruit providing sustenance.

Sustenance producing life;

Praise Him with all rejoicing for the giving of life.

BROKEN HEARTED

My heart is broken,

Torn apart as by a lion devouring a fresh kill to stave off starvation.

Utterly annihilated by a mother who poured out revenge for the traumas of another life lost.

Each attack unpicking a thread of a magnificent tapestry one knot at a time; each word possessing the power of death.

Turning the soul and twisting,

Suffocating until the desire to live ebbs away, and death's door holds a bleak fascination.

Bruises and blood mix together, then a tender touch in all the wrong places brings forth a snipers calm, steady hand;

A perfect aim, unnerving explosions of a controlled visceral rage.

An anger that if unconstrained will build higher prison walls to hold it back.

Bleak dawn proceeds bleak dawn; black ice, dark and hard,

Cold, buried deep, but, not deep enough. Nowhere is ever deep enough.

THIRTY

Just as the strummer plucks out the notes on a guitar that vibrates with the same rhythm of the heart,[1]

So the pulse that passes blood around the body is a gift of the Holy Spirit.

Oh my God, I cry out for you in the agony of this life. Can you lift me up from the grave and put me into prince's robes?

Heal my soul, my body, my mind.

Can I ever be as sorry as I think I should? Will it take all of my life to make things right?

Your anger is but for a moment and though my weeping may endure for a night, as surely as the sun rises, joy comes in the morning.

Hide not your face from my troubled soul as I seek your redemption,

Your gift, your favour to stand over me like a banner,

Your word declares me to be strong.

---

[1] This poem relates to Psalm 30 (hence title Thirty).

WHAT SCAFFOLD?

There wasn't much scaffolding around to help us grow up straight.

Mum would take me to phone boxes to slide a long blade into the coin slot, dislodging the contents coin after coin into her bag of poverty.

Her tortured emotions would pour out in screams and shouts of rage and frustration. Bursts of red-hot volcanic temper spewing out for all to see.

Unavailable to selflessly love her child, to give protection and boundaries, the child learns to protect itself.

Learning to function alone, self- sufficient, getting by on fragments of a twisted form of distorted love.

Eventually, learning much later that only God's love is capable of sustenance and that His light offers a sense of being absent from early in life's journey, He has brought me this far.

STILL NOT THERE

For most of my life I have been denying those feelings of helplessness; believing in something so distant.

Not you, nor me.

All of the promises that I have made and broken turn to haunt me.

There is nothing left but a broken darkness inside that can only hint at the dreams and desires that once lived within me.

As I gaze out of the window, pulse running, I don't see the face I've been looking for—

Is He so far away?

I am panting on my knees, beside the brook. Unable to look for His face,

Too lost to sense His grace.

As much as I want the past not to exist, it still does. And, as much as I want to belong, I can't see the point of a future spent alone.

There is nothing left,

All I can feel are the cold hard winds tearing at my lost soul. Where are you?

One day I will not be able to feel this pain, this rejection any longer.

The shadows of me that wanted to see won't come into focus any more.

Take it all away, all I can see is this cruel haunting of who you wanted me to be.

Left lost and broken,

Without a token of your great love.

The bitter cold of the frost is biting deep, paradise is lost,

Lost to me as my face sinks into a deep abyss; no gentle kiss to comfort me.

Where is my Shulamite at night as the darkness grips me tightly?

Take it all away, shake it off, let go of me. I cannot hear the music,

Is it in my head, this hopeless dread? My bed is cold and lonely, stony quiet.

The enveloping of the darkness of the night bites; still not there.

FREEFALL

It feels like the wind blows cold, like the winds of the world blow cold on me.

Who do I give myself to? Don't cling on to me, I can't hold on to you too!

Free falling, tumbling down over and over, never sure which way is up.

Can't see the horizon, eyes streaming shut.

If you love me then help me, so that I am not held down by who I used to be,

That's not me anymore. Don't shut the door,

It feels like all of my screams have gone unheard, with the weight of the world upon my slender shoulders, I wait.

The truth will set us free; and the sound of His voice will bring comfort in free fall.

If you'll let me, I will love you the way that He shows me how to love you.

Forgive me, for you are not alone.

EDGES

I was awoken to something new, something lying dormant; perhaps even dead.

As the autumn of my years ebbed away you changed me and my outlook.

I burn with curiosity.

I learned not to fake-take, put the mask away, put me last.

Not easy when the zoo that produced me left competitive edges.

Not slow to go forward, a mistake to make, when haste is repaid with another dead dream.

I know that if I place my hope on things above that I will be safe.

Peace prevails, breaks out in all directions. Love ensues,

I cannot share what I have not got.

I can hide away in my cave, close my eyes and cry.

Played that game too many times.

The hearts warming glow just visible in the snow; edges obscuring, hope springing, eternity shows the way.

SOARING BEAUTY

Despite myself, the Holy Spirit gave me an unexpected new name.

I had only just enough belief to speak it out.

Protected, encouraged, nurtured under the Eagle's wing;

Soaring high to see things His way: from a higher, wider perspective.

No longer grounded but lifted, elevated; a living metaphor for His healing love.

Yokes easier, strongholds challenged.

Loving possibilities emerging, protecting, hoping, persevering. Yet aware of self-destruction.

Soaring on the word of God—out of harm's way for good.

From surrender, beauty emerges with a depth, bringing light that I let shine through my brokenness.

Standing in awe of you, my soul transforms,

The suspension of the mask assured.

All that I am stands in you and your goodness embraces all,

Leaving nothing unseen.

FEAR OF FLYING

To get yourself from one distant place to another, it is sometimes necessary to fly. During the mid-nineteen nighties, myself and two friends pitched up at Chichester aerodrome and took a flight in a single engine Piper aircraft along the coastal areas of Sussex, England.

As we approached the airport on the return journey and with a closing speed of close to 300MPH (483KPH), the pilot was forced to make an emergency manoeuvre to avoid a mid-air collision with another light aircraft coming in the opposite direction.

We all survived to tell the tale.

I learned that sometimes evasive manoeuvres are required to avoid catastrophe, a stumbling designed by the enemy to kill and to maim. Had we died that day I would have perished unsaved, not knowing my Lord and saviour. So for the next ten years I adopted a fear of flying, until God used another close call in a plane to cur my fear.

On a business trip our plane was caught in a mighty cross wind. As we came in to land, it was all bent out of shape and twisted by high winds. But we were safe; and I was healed of my fear of flying.

Healed and saved from above, massive power massive love.

ECHO FINDER

I tell you, let your tears flow, and let your past go.

To find the fullness of love and life, first you must lose it,

Give it up, pass up all of the trappings of privilege.

Then you will find that His massive power and His massive love conquer all to heal and save from above.

So, let your tears flow, let your past go.

Invisible to the naked eye, and as soft as the third or fourth echo in a cave, is His gentle voice, seeking out your heart.

So, let the tears flow, let the past go, let it go, let it go.

As the water level rises, healing breaks out.

Healed and saved from above, massive power, massive love.

Arise, as Christ was raised to life, drop off those old grave clothes, put on the purple robes and receive your double blessing.

An abundance that will chase you down as you step out to take dominion over your inheritance.

Let your tears flow, let the past go, finding the echo, found the echo.

CARVING CANYONS

As the smoke belches from a fire rising upward into the atmosphere, particles of pollution effuse into the air—entering the body in the air that we breathe.

Along with the years' that the locusts have stolen, wrong choices have kept me supping at poisonous streams,

Only seen in the granting of a graceful redemption.

How long will it take for healthy fruits to ripen for the eating?

The sense of loss is palpable, like gazing out over the vast expanse of the Grand Canyon with its river of melted snow,

Purified waters carving canyons through the boulders.

The sheer power of purity magnified by the distance to the canyon floor where the river drives its rapids.

Watching, as the imagination endeavours to determine the source of the design, the wonder of creation.

Stars are imploding—sucking in vast darkness—

Incalculable; neither seen nor felt on our tiny dot.

Yet, I know His love is vaster than these.

HIDING CLOUD FORMATIONS

I stop the watch, panting, aching from the run with
the same time recorded that was common in earlier
times.

Not being a chicken of spring any longer I wonder
how can this be?

I lift up my eyes to the sky and see the unique cloud
formations hiding the face of the answer to my
question.

An unassuming collection of numbers.

Is it for me to guess how to lift myself out of a broken
mess?

Only Daddy's hand can bless and deliver the desires
of the heart in their time.

If I have any humility I am equally steeled for the
possibilities

That He could bring along at any time.

Shall I calmly refuse possessive obsession, aware of
the damage, treading lightly?

LADY DEATH

Today I am safe and secure knowing that His love knows no end.

It was not always thus.

Two months ahead of my baptism, my now ex-wife elected to take the life that was growing inside of her.

Deep tribulations followed, guilt did not assuage my part.

The devil's work twisted her inside-out for years, in figure eights, up one minute, down the next. Peace was elusive.

In time I was released from this poisonous relationship.

The Lord taking ashes and torment—praise His Holy name,

There is no refrain that I can muster to describe this murder.

Utterly disgraced, shamed and abandoned.

Healing comes only at a gradual pace, no race to face grace; down with my frowning face.

Grateful that mercy triumphs over judgement and a meeting awaits me in heaven.

HEALING FULNESS

Your fullness is healing me; your truth sets me free.

These dead, dry bones are taking up life as you move me towards you.

My soul heals—becomes more whole—as I wade out into the river;

The water level is rising almost imperceptibly initially.

Then, it rises and rises and you show me that the shifting of the sands has given over to something stronger,

Stable, no longer insouciant, no longer blown so readily by the winds—change has wrought a shape solidified like a sword,

Hammered a thousand times into a fine blade by the smith,

Layer upon layer of refinement building up a foundation of to be established in the heat of battle.

I wrestle for a time with what to do, then I always remember that it is you

Who guides and leads in holy ways.

I am not overlooked or forgotten; I am precious and loved much.

PRISON BREAK

My Lord, my Lord, how I yearn for you to bring my soul up out of the prison,

A self-imposed exile awaiting the opening of heaven.

As you pour out blessings, the increase, the overflow brings profound restoration.

Physical and spiritual repair, oneness.

I have not yet gotten to the point of saying I do,

As I wait for you to cause me to know your will; which way I should walk.

As I lift up my soul to you, a deep black hole opens in front of me.

Without a diversion I will be swallowed up again.

Teach me a new song, teach me your will, sit me still.

My eyes seek you expectantly, looking your way for answers that reflect your glorious splendour.

Teach me patience.

Here I am, down on my knees again as you draw near.

I know that I am desperate for you, drench my soul in mercy. Help me, help me.

HEART MAP

There is a season of realisation, a gradual understanding,

A revelation that I don't know what I don't know — and what I do know is useless.

The season holds tribulations, a multiplication of the number of chambers of the heart,

Needing healing, soothing touch of the father's love.

Truly, it is a mystery to me, the intricate mapping of the heart.

I thought I knew every area, could describe every nuance, every chamber.

But, as I cry out in submission, sensitivity deepens, tears flow.

The night creeps by, bit by bit. I'm keeping some things inside, so close to giving up.

Faith is so hard to find. The sighs come with the tears in the dark.

This is how I learn to be pure again — offer up a bruised heart to the designer, who allows the cries of my heart,

He knows me, shapes me, loves me.

HE TEACHES ME

It is a miracle that I am still alive. No doubt.

Restored to life with a clarity that belies the evidence of my demise. So grateful that God intervened.

He created rock and roll for me. The beats soothe my troubled soul.

They beat to the rhythm of the blood pumped around my body by my heart.

Gods provision trumps all expectations. He's teaching me a lesson.

Aim higher—change is everywhere—pointless to resist—nothing remains the same—transitions reign.

If love is a choice, please teach me to choose wisely.

Teach me not to be afraid of my own brilliance, help me to find ways to express it for your glory; for you have made me an overcomer.

Show me, encourage me, to put down the negative, darker sides, how to embrace life fully.

Teach me to be a better coach, a better keeper of my gate.

Increase patience to let me see what you have in store just around the corner.

SILENT SCREAM

The dreams of childhood were shattered by a parent who served time for his crimes.

Though a year's incarceration these days of child protection would surely be more like life.

A girl of eleven, a boy of seven, a girl of seven and a boy of five survived; kept alive by the Holy Spirit.

The system was down—didn't help with counselling or anything tender; no loving emotional care or protection.

Mother took over persecution duties out of rage and anger and alcohol dependency.

These were post-war parents, not very bright, steeped in poverty of all shades.

They beat, they robbed and mugged and touched in all the wrong places.

A strong silent scream was the only way to bear their faces—only in death could I start to heal and discover forgiveness.

Decades later, compassionate love for them and their plight emerges. Thank you God.

Thank you that I stayed out of crime and prison, let down by the system.

COMFORTING TEARS

The sound of their cries could be heard all around the house.

He liked to imagine great big yellow tractors with great big wheels turning slowly tracking through the mud.

She held the hand of an elder sister for comfort as the lights went out and the games began for the night.

The smell of the carpet was dusty and old, not even the biting cold could bring a hint of relief from the thief in the night.

Can the cries still be heard, does the house remember?

This far away will someone come and save the day or do we have to wait till the day that He takes our cries and turns our mourning into dancing.

Will He take away our sadness and turn it into joy?

Will there come a time with no more tears?

With grace in our hearts and pretty flowers in our hair—not this day, but, not far away.

See into my eyes, before the fire dies.

RESTORER

Can the sweeter side of me survive the debauchery?

Will anyone ever see the real me? Is the man that I am going to me all that far away from the one that I used to be?

I recall at age three as violence rained down on me,

Looking into his eyes as they narrowed into slits.

Wondering when the love would come.

Hey dad! What's that running down my legs?

Tears aren't yellow I'm falling, falling between the waves,

Can't breathe properly, terror invades. Where is He who saves?

I crawl off into a cave for a generation or two as the fog readies itself to lift.

He who saves, heals, and restores was there, right with me in the darkest days.

Never leaving me, keeping my sanity.

Sane, keeping the pain relieved, He gave me a new heart,

More than one new start, and a bit of time to play my part as me.

THE AXE HEAD

My feet have been dragging in the silt; my path littered with stumbling blocks, the waters way over my head.

Daring not to breathe too deeply, vision impaired as I write this letter to you. Now, you won't understand a word that is in it, but you'll get it long before you die.

Oh, how I have longed to even permit myself to long for you; my eyes stream.

The loneliness has gone; joyful are the sounds of your cries.

The giggles of your voice reach me and my heart beats harder and reaches for the sky.

As your arms are lifted, waiting expectantly, I lift you up high into the sky.

And, I kneel down and I wait till I can see you again.

Praying that I won't forget blocks that I have stumbled upon.

Elisha raised an axe head in a miracle and the child that he prophesied when dead was bought back to life.

Now like Elisha, God is using you to bring life abundant, delicious, unexpected, delightful life; give it to me.

LOST IN YOU

It's not always easy to see when things are not right;

Smothered by sexual need that fades as the days go by.

It doesn't have to be this way; the good things, they can come to you too.

Pretty as a blooming lily with flare and abundant colours.

Sharp witted and smart love that it seemed was once impossible, dead.

Those memories can't feed the needs of a heart released from the chains of pain.

To look upon a happier vista, to dare to check the time and see that it hasn't yet run out.

Not altogether. There is still a godly chunk to plant a tree or two, to watch them grow.

Well, it's time to hit my knees, to give thanks for these revelations.

Bow my head and close my eyes—lost in you.

SEPTEMBER

I don't like September all that much. Maybe it's the change to the season, maybe its some other reason.

All of the things that grow begin a slow turn to mush, in the rush toward colder days and shorter nights.

Is my detection of the outpouring stopping? Still needing to receive Him, be renewed be refreshed;

Restored in winter, invigorated, renewed—receive healing as your body becomes mine.

Then I remember the abominations of the mind and of the flesh and I begin to feel far, far away.

Even as you say 'Son of Man lift your head,' the dread in my heart keeps me from looking.

You are the Lord Almighty who forgets nothing; I fear you as you prepare to lay your vengeance upon me.

There is nowhere to hide, my pride makes me ashamed. Will my restoration to First Love bring joy?

Will your majesty help me to lift up my eye and strengthen my bones, reinvigorate a life marked by the savage passage of time?

Help me, lengthen my shadow. I pray that there are sufficient days left to yet praise your glory and your faithfulness.

NOT MY REFRAIN

Can anyone write a refrain just like Kurt Cobain? I couldn't bring my brain to entertain that sound again, and again.

Being from the rainy side of the pond, we grew fond of My Generation,

Whilst sitting on The Rock contemplating Wire and Angels and an eternal thread of post-war dread.

The Yellow Submarine ran aground on a jagged little mound of brown sugar.

Did sucking on the pipe change the sight of those internal frights, was a vain full of smack the only way to attack back?

Was raging anger a comforting blanket to hide inside?

Did death bring the relief from the thief who stole the whole show, would Keith and the Ox still like to out-fox the Giver of the gifts that were left behind?

When all is said and done, we can't outlive the time we are given. No amount of manly strength can overcome the grave,

Hear and Now, the last note of Brilliant Blues will come to take me, to pay me back for those refrains that I listened to that weren't mine to choose. Say goodbye, it's time.

RIGHT STEP

As I know that all of my pride renders me useless in the Kingdom of God,

I am charged to fall to my knees and pray for understanding and wisdom.

As to fall back into destruction, arms carry a deadly burden for me.

So, I prepare my preparations and surrender to the Spirit's guidance of the steps that He wants me to take.

Committing with integrity, my word to the Lord; for He has made it all possible Himself.

In mercy and in truth the air that I breathe comes to me.

He grants me a great redemption for my sin, for my sins are many and great. A man's heart may plan the way that he wants to go,

But, only the Lord directs the steps of his feet.

May my lips not lead me into betrayal—

Preserve my soul Lord.

SECTION 3

SOMEONE TO SHARE WITH

WAITING

Jesus creates the space for my soul to rest, to find peace.

He has raised up a helpmate from the hill country to cushion the blow and to share the shelter that He has provided;

Bringing a depth of character, a smile and a laugh that you can detect from the next county.

Tender hearted and cheerful, made of strong stuff with the love of the Lord a woman of God.

She rests on His rock seeking intimacy to work out the way to hear His voice,

To hear Him say that she has His blessing.

Waiting in hope waiting in loving patience, will she detect the wings of the dove?

The Father's blessings were here yesterday and the Bible tells me they won't go away.

So, joy has been released to keep me company; as I wait.

BITTER SWEET

Your lips are like the fragrance and taste of a peach.

Your eyes light up big and dark open and seeking.

Your kisses are at once tender and urgent like the world ends today.

Your hair is flowing like the blossom of summer flowers, alluring and enticing hinting at hidden depths.

Observing you, my breathing changes caught in my throat.

Your movement graceful and light, rhythmic.

A wave of the tenderest love is overwhelming me;

Wrapping me up in your arms it feels as if destiny has arrived,

And the deepest bliss seeps into my being.

Did my Father ever tell me it could be like this?

Am I dreaming someone else's dream, is this happening to me?

When you smile at me your face shines and your eyes gleam.

Catching glimpses of you regarding me from afar, my heart leaps.

MAN UP

Nothing happens to you that God does not permit or allow. All things.

I have been looking for love in all the wrong faces.

His grace has shown me that it is never too late to have a happy childhood—start whenever you would like to.

Despair is a prideful thing,

Head knowledge gives the heart consumption.

God does not mind which wife I choose,

He minds that I exercise my will to grow from a childish perspective.

My real self, my real me, will not emerge when I am looking to find it,

It can only be found in Him.

It is God's intention that we are to be lovers, help me to stop hiding and exercising self-preservation,

In Jesus' name.

If the fruit that you have found in the forest was not that for which you were searching, or expected to find,

Put the fruit back and find another.

IS IT YOU?

There was a time when you asked me to come to my last first date with you.

I was already there with my slicked back hair,

Pulse elevated, trying not to stare.

Wait, wait, she said, I like to procrastinate.

I hate to procrastinate, knowing it may already be too late in life to bring a wife along to share the rest of this journey of life.

Seeing eye-to-eye on so many things it was hard for me to see the strings,

One little lie is all that it took to place the foundation into a state of shattered shock.

Forgive me Daddy, this fruit tastes bitter,

Will you permit me another?

An oasis in the wilderness brings water and life,

The cleansing, clearing of the garden brings a step out of the wilderness toward wonder.

WHERE IS YOUR PRESENCE?

The tears will not stop running down my face, collecting in pools of water and snot in the crevice of my neck.

My stomach churns, seeking a trace of your sweet perfume, to embrace a memory of your face.

The way that you flick your hair leaves a scent on the air so fleeting not alleviating my grieving.

The wrong song comes on—again—reminding of those summer times.

Now winter is here and I miss you dear.

Will you return or will you leave me to learn another lesson for a season,

For a reason beyond any comprehension,

Love lost?

The radiators cannot bring warmth to the empty chambers of my heart,

Utterly devoid and broken again.

As much as I wanted you, I still sit on the cold underside of the covers dreaming that day light will soon return and chase away the chills of the night.

ROMANS 8:28

Where is your presence? Where is your warm embrace?

Have I lost all trace of it?

Deep water is all around, such deep waters that I could be in a dream,

With search-lights looking all around for my last first date.

My best mate.

If I come looking again for you, will you want to be found?

Have you flown off to a faraway land to find paradise another way?

I know it was never rational, my love for a national from a far off land in transition.

It was all in my thoughts—that I could bridge the gap and elevate Him who made all things possible.

Would I could remain straight and true, to me and to you, for you make all things good for those who love you.

URGENT NOT HASTE

Like a grain of sand at the seashore or an atom out at sea, you could easily pass me by.

Have you played me and betrayed me, flayed me till I bleed?

Stomach churning, yearning, sulphuric acid burning, will I ever feel a loving warm embrace again?

Walk on the beach in the rain?

Be bested at chess, turn order into mess?

I must confess it was all me — 100% responsibility.

Was my urgency transparent to see?

Maybe I was too far away, wearing my heart on my sleeve,

A bit of a giveaway.

Labels, logo's and motto's won't save the day,

They just fade away.

The only rock of any value is the Rock of Ages

Who breaks our self-imposed cages,

Drives away the cravings,

Transforms chaos into a world of possibility; in me to see.

PURPOSEFUL DISTRACTION

Why is it that a good partner is so hard to find?

The machinations of hell's bells toll all around drowning out the still small voice—am I listening?

The absence of comfort and joy, a clue;

Will my lover's eyes ever gaze into mine?

Will I weep lacking courage, full of the problems that were made inside my own head?

The soul aches to have done things another way, but, then He couldn't use me in that way.

I didn't survive because I am fit; I survived because I'm not. There is nothing to come back from.

The foundations are stronger, there all along to settle upon in the times of distraction.

To work upon a fraction of the fragmented distant purpose—distractions to my life's action.

MY STONE

Instead of finding what I wanted, I found myself in second place;

I ran the race and found myself just waiting by the phone;

Lonely but maybe not on my own.

Pity, party ending, feeling alone. Will I ever feel the tender touch of love?

I still want to be the someone you are with; the one for me in this life.

To be that illusive last first date, your best mate.

It's not too late and I don't believe in fate,

I know I can wait. I'm just not that good at it.

Fingers tap, a drummer beats the drum, and surely everybody needs someone?

Who cares if you are alone, the last one to find that upturned stone,

For you to pick up, to polish, and to cherish.

To fold two into one at last; fold away that comfort zone and finally,

Stop going it alone.

WOULD YOU?

If I could find something good to die for, would the beauty of life and all creation continue to evade me?

If I could walk over Happy Valley with the snow on the ground—

Without an icy blast of winter wind—

Would I be able to see the beauty of that vista?

If I could only pin down the moment when it all goes right,

Could I save something for the time when it all goes wrong?

If I could surrender those parts that dwell in the dark recesses,

Would she take my hand as we stroll through the valleys?

As the sun sets on another day, can I find a way to give up the fleshly ways leading me to stray?

Stray into cold water which freezes my heart, rendering me unable to contemplate taking part with another heart;

This journey of life—another new start?

FIGMENTS OF FANTASY

I am trying to increase the population of this town.

But, all I've got is a nagging sensation that I have been here before, running out of time.

Accidents happen, but, nothing happens by accident.

So, here I lay broken hearted, contemplating a conveyor-belt of lost opportunities.

Fragments now of a fantasy that wasn't ready to mature, to be fulfilled.

Still yearning and burning, will Ethelred the unready ever truly be ready?

The breaking of the alabaster jar was a signal of intent,

But, in this life a man doesn't live by bread alone.

This is a reality. As real as it gets.

And, God doesn't mind who I choose as a wife, He wants me to be positive in my choice.

So, as I let the tears flow and I let the past go, the fragments of fantasy dissolve and are placed behind the boundary wall.

Soul ties severed, purity compromised a little less each day.

READY HEART?

You know, I have been actively preparing my heart for you.

If I am still around this time next year, will I have done enough for you to want to share your heart with mine?

Can the thoughts that I have been processing enable conjoining with you?

Will the angels be rejoicing at the sounds of our laughter together?

I cannot see a way to do this alone—

Bearing my heart to you has been an act of faith.

I have not heard that I will be a part of what we have made.

I just hold out my hands and hope that the day will arrive.

Trusting that I will not have to destroy every thought I have had along the way,

I will not regret picking up a strange new fruit.

My hands will not stop clapping and giving thanks and praising.

POLUTED HOPE

My heart is broken. I tell you that I love you. Yet, I don't know why I trust you.

I still believe it's you and me till the end of time. Where did I go wrong?

You let me down, was I ever good enough, did you write me off?

Could you see right through me, was my toxicity too high?

Was my impurity a bitter taste to you? I'm just another work in progress,

Turning a mess into something less awkward to deal with.

Is there a chamber in my heart that lets the sewage pour out?

Did you suck it up and wince? Will I wonder till the end of time?

Torn away from you, have you pulled away to let restoration plat its way.

I sit here in this darkened room praying for breakthrough.

God let your fire fall down. I cannot see. Have I any right to?

BEAUTIFUL DAY

Oh, how I long for you to wrap your loving arms around me.

Pull on some jeans, put on some boots and let's ride up into the rolling hills of the Downs.

The engine purring away like my soul on this beautiful day.

I am one.

No wind, no rain just the wonder of a private refrain,

Allowing the reign of heaven to rain down.

The Lords refreshing outpouring over us, sublime.

Synchronicity as hearts beat in unity.

The beauty of the landscape catching the breath encouraging awe in the One who made it all.

Pouring out blessing from an open heaven.

Captured in the moment in His bubble of loving protection.

Spirit filled location following us from bend to bend,

Our unseen best friend seizing the moment of joy to dwell with His children.

LOST

You were a precious gift sent from Heaven.

I didn't want to send you back.

Will I be present in your future, as I wish to be in your present?

I can see your presence in my past,

It all went by so fast; I'm sorry.

Did the Lord want you to change me some way?

Becoming more like Him from inside out is really all I know to do.

Hold myself accountable to the light,

To examine what might need developing and what might need transforming.

Forgive myself for your loss, lift up my chin.

Not casting down my countenance now as I feel I'll just drown.

In my sorrow the silence breaks;

I know there is nothing that I can change, only He can heal.

LAST FIRST LOVE

That dress looks really nice on you.

The colours and the patterns compliment you.

The way that the light dances on your hair and light up your eyes

When you smile, delights.

To behold your elegant hands;

Fingers framed by perfect coloured nails.

You walk with an ease and grace.

As the breeze wafts your hair into my face,

I catch a glimpse of your perfume and my heart skips a beat.

As you take my hand in yours and we walk in step, no haste.

Unity detected, far off, a gift.

Its absence so swift to mark the end of something.

Do we ignore the trend, play with a friend, ask God to send us another answer.

Go to the spring for refreshing and renewal and on bended knee seek restoration to first love.

REFLECTIONS

Do not blame things on what you have been through.

Take a close look in the mirror and reflect what it is you are into.

If your focus is trained on the trouble and strife from your former life,

How do you expect the love of your life to emerge?

Hopes, wants and aspirations can all be deflected if inner healing isn't permitted to bring attention

To the things that you don't want to mention.

A cry in the dark to the maker of your shelter can start to shed light on your plight.

Don't do it alone, how can you do it alone?

Recline into the Rock of your salvation and wait.

Pray for patience; revelation comes.

Faithfully He will show the way for you, take your hand and take you deeper into Him.

Trust He won't sleep till the promise He has made to you is revealed.

Be still, soak in Him.

TAKE ME AWAY

Take me away goes the refrain. Where do you want to go, do you even know? Why are you wrestling in the season of resting?

Yes, but, I do know where it is that I want to go. It is just that being solo has got to go.

Time for a duet in the snow, as we ski long and low. Ice skating in the winter freeze, walking through the autumn leaves.

It's time for the soul to sing the rejoicing sounds of a duet walking in step.

Awake my soul, to see that it is no longer a solo trip here and there for me.

The elated cry from the inside is that He has set things to right, made His timing right.

There are only two seats in the car and the spare looks a little empty for now.

All shiny and clean, ready to take you away to listen to the waves crashing in the sea.

Kicking pebbles on the beach, a seat for you and for me.

NEW LIFE

Today I picked up the green flag and waived it over my church family.

The green flag represents New Life and I have never waved anything else.

As Daddy wants me to step into reliability, focus on the family,

I find myself single and hesitating to choose positively

Between being a boy-friend or living in the responsibility of being a husband.

Tested and trying times my flesh is so weak and my stomach aches—

Lord help me to hand over to you the hidden dirty rags that I have tried to hide.

Help me to discern why there is a mismatch from your divine love to me and my love to others.

My keeper of the gate, my helper, who is she going to be?

This is my life; am I everything that you want me to be?

Lord give me the courage of a young lion to take back that which the enemy has stolen.

Forgive me in my manipulation and lasting disobedience,

Prepare a way for me of resounding clarity,

Let not the fog of history's mistakes bite too deeply.

Let not my thirst and hunger,

My burning for companionship,

Deflect me from your truth in my life.

Let your love reign o'er me, let it rain, let it reign, let it rain.